Explaining
Prayer

Joyce Huggett

Sovereign World

Scripture quotations are taken from the
The Holy Bible, New International Version.
© Copyright 1973, 1978, 1984 International Bible Society.
Published by Hodder & Stoughton.

JB – Jerusalem Bible. © Copyright 1966 Darton Longman & Todd.

LB – Living Bible. © Copyright 1971 Tyndale House Publishers.

GNB – Good News Bible.
© Copyright 1966, 1971 American Bible Society, New York.

ISBN: 1 85240 065 X

This Sovereign World book is distributed in North America by Renew Books,
a ministry of Gospel Light, Ventura, California, USA. For a free catalog of resources
from Renew Books/Gospel Light, please contact your Christian supplier
or call 1-800-4-GOSPEL.

SOVEREIGN WORLD LIMITED
P.O. Box 777, Tonbridge, Kent TN11 0ZS, England.

Typeset and printed in the UK by Sussex Litho Ltd, Chichester, West Sussex.

Contents

For

Martin and Susan

with thanks

Introduction

I started this book in Cyprus where I live. I continued it in England where I was born. And I put the finishing touches to it in New Zealand while I was working with Christians from a variety of countries: Japan, Thailand, Papua New Guinea, Tonga, to mention a few.

I, too, work for the Church overseas. My husband and I are Mission Partners with Interserve. We lead prayer retreats for Christians in leadership. So when our friend Chris Mungeam invited me to write this short book, I was delighted – especially when he said: 'Not everyone who reads it will have learned English as their first language. Imagine that you are writing to pastors overseas who speak their own language fluently but who may have learned English later in life.'

I have had the privilege of paying short visits to Kenya and Tanzania as well as Poland and met with pastors in this situation. It is with these friends in my mind that I have penned these pages.

In addition to keeping the language simple, I have included three drawings to help readers to understand my train of thought. I am grateful to Kerry Davies for drawing these for me.

I feel excited as I think of this little book reaching far-flung corners of the world. I feel even more excited as I think of Christians in many countries exploring God's gift of prayer. The words which I have often prayed while writing the manuscript are these: *'Our Father...'* – the first two words of the prayer Jesus taught us. As I say these words, they remind me that we are all one big family. God's family. They remind me, too, that prayer is the cement which holds us together in love. So as we continue our prayer journey, perhaps we can remember to pray for one another from time to time? That way we shall be drawn together within the love of God.

Joyce Huggett, May 1993

1

What is Prayer?

'What is prayer?' That is a question I asked a group of Christians at a School of Prayer I was leading on one occasion. Each person gave a different answer. So the list looked like this:

Prayer is:

    talking to God

    listening to God

    friendship with God

    trusting God

Prayer is:

    being loved by God

    being found by God

    being held by God

    being guided by God

Prayer is:

    confessing our sins

    repenting

    forgiving others

    receiving God's forgiveness

Prayer is:

    being silent before God

    praising God

    worshipping God

    meeting God

Prayer is:

    opening the door of our heart to God

    meeting God

    recognising that God lives inside us

Prayer is:

    fighting God's Enemy – Satan.

The Bible's Teaching on Prayer

The list was long. But was it accurate? In order to discover whether our ideas came from our own heads or from the Bible, we looked at Jesus' teaching on the subject and watched the way he prayed to his Heavenly Father. Next we examined the Bible's teaching on the Holy Spirit, the One who helps us to pray. When we had done this, we came to the conclusion that everyone's answer was right. Just as many peaks make a mountain, so prayer is made up of all the things we mentioned and many more. This is what makes prayer so exciting. This is why prayer is sometimes called an adventure – a journey into God.

As you read this book, imagine that we are on this journey together and that, as we travel, our understanding of prayer may grow. Then, at every stage of the journey our hearts will overflow with praise to the God who has given us this wonderful gift – the gift of prayer.

2

Preparing to Pray

One day, while Jesus' disciples were watching him pray, they said to him: *"Lord, teach **us** to pray."*

In some ways this was a strange thing to ask. These men had been praying ever since they were children. Their mothers and fathers and teachers in the Synagogue would have taught them to pray. But they seem to have seen in Jesus a kind of prayer they had not experienced before.

Jesus had given them the privilege of hearing him talk to his Father:

> *'I praise you, Father, Lord of heaven and earth...'*
> (Matthew 11:25)

> *'Father, I thank you for hearing my prayer. I know indeed that you always hear me...'*   (John 11:42 JB)

And they had seen him at prayer – at his Baptism, early in the morning (Mark 1:35), late at night (Matthew 14:23), sometimes all through the night (Luke 6:12). They knew that his relationship with God was warm and close as well as reverent. In response to their request Jesus gave them a list of instructions which helped them to understand what prayer really means and how to go about it.

In this chapter we shall begin to look together at this teaching.

> *'When you pray'*, Jesus told them, *'go into your room, close the door and pray to your Father, who is unseen. Then your Father, who sees what is done in secret, will reward you.'*
> (Matthew 6:6)

All kinds of practical suggestions hide in this verse. The first is: find a prayer place.

In some ways, this suggestion is a strange one because Jesus himself once made it clear to his followers that he had no one place he could call home:

> *'Foxes have holes and birds of the air have nests, but the Son of Man has nowhere to lay his head.'*   (Matthew 8:20)

Even so, Jesus practised what he preached and found places where he could pray to his Father in secret:

> *'Very early in the morning, while it was still dark, Jesus got up, left the house and went off to a solitary place, where he prayed.'*   (Mark 1:35)

Did he sit by the Sea of Galilee and watch the rising sun paint the world pink while he prayed? Or did he climb the hills and find a place to pray on the grassy slopes? We know that, when he was in Galilee, he went often to the hills to pray:

> *'...he went up into the hills by himself to pray. When evening came, he was there alone.'*   (Matthew 14:22, 23 JB)

> *'Jesus went out into the hills to pray, and spent the night praying to God.'*   (Luke 6:12)

And when he was in Jerusalem, we know that he used to go often to the Garden of Gethsemane to meet with his Father. That is why Judas knew where to find him on the night before he was crucified.

Like Jesus, many Christians today have no room where they can go to be alone with God. They have to find another place. I think of the Christians I once talked to in Singapore. One girl lived in a small flat with nine other members of her family. When I asked her where she prayed she said: 'I sit under a tree on my way to the bus stop each morning. That's where I meet God.' Another said, 'I go to the office really early and have my Quiet

10

Time with God before anyone else arrives.'

These testimonies helped me to realise that people who really want to pray will find a place where they can meet with God in secret. They find a place because Jesus suggested that they should. Then they discover the value of this prayer place. When we pray in the same place every day for weeks and months and years we visit it with a sense of expectancy that God will, indeed, meet with us. Very often his presence can be felt there in all its power and holiness. There we discover him assuring us that he is anxious to listen to us and to speak to us.

Pray to Your Father

'When you have found a prayer place, remember that you are praying to a Father who loves you', Jesus seems to say: 'This, then is how you should pray: *"Our Father in heaven..."*' (Matthew 6:9).

Whenever Jesus prayed, he called God 'Father'.

The word Jesus uses for 'Father' is 'Abba' – 'Daddy' – the first word a child learns to say. A word born of trust.

Two children in the Middle East helped me to understand what Jesus meant when he encouraged us to pray in this way. One was a little boy on a bus.

The little boy was sitting on his father's lap. The bus was crowded and it was late. The child was obviously very tired. After we had travelled for a few miles, the boy looked into his father's face, stroked his beard lovingly, whispered the word 'Abba!' several times, then placed his head on his father's chest and fell fast asleep. While his son slept, the father looked at him with love in his eyes.

The other was a small child by a swimming pool. He was being helped into the water by his big sisters but his face said: 'I don't know whether to laugh or cry.' Then a man appeared. 'Abba! Abba!' the boy called. The child's father went to him. They played in the pool together and enjoyed their swim. The boy's fear left him. He now showed no signs of crying, only of laughing. While Abba was near, he was happy.

11

'That's the kind of love and trust Jesus wants us to have in our Heavenly Father,' I thought.

Come with Confidence

When we know that love is what God is and that he delights in us in the same way as good mothers and fathers enjoy their children, we can come to him with confidence, knowing that he will listen to our prayers and answer them. Jesus reminds us of this:

> *'When you pray, go away by yourself, all alone, and shut the door behind you and pray to your Father secretly, and your Father, who knows your secrets, will reward you... Remember, your Father knows exactly what you need even before you ask him!'* (Matthew 6:6,8 Living Bible)

I like the way Jesus reminds us that our Heavenly Father knows our secrets and that he also knows exactly what we need before we ask him. This means that we can pray with an expectation that God will not only listen to us, he will help us in the way which is best for us at any given moment.

It also means that we do not have to pray long prayers. The Jews used to think that if their prayers were long and loud, God would answer them more quickly. But Jesus made it clear that praying like this is unnecessary:

> *"When you pray, do not keep on babbling like pagans, for they think that they will be heard because of their many words. Do not be like them, for your Father knows what you need before you ask him.'* (Matthew 6:7, 8)

Remember God is Holy

In this verse Jesus is showing us that God loves us even more than good parents love their children. He reads the deepest secrets of our hearts and wants to meet those needs because he loves us so much. In other words, although God's love is even more beautiful than the love good parents have for their children, at the same time, God is quite different from our earthly parents. This is because the heavenly Father is holy. The word 'holy' means different, special, set apart. So there has never, ever been anyone like God. He is 'Other'.

This is good news for the people who have grown up with parents who have not been as loving as parents should be. Maybe their father was cruel or unkind. The word 'father' for such people seems rather an ugly, frightening word. But the Bible reminds us that God is not like that. God is love. Therefore God is like a loving father and a loving mother all in one. The Psalmist puts it this way:

> *'As a father has compassion on his children, so the Lord has compassion on those who fear him.'*   (Psalm 103:13)

Isaiah says:

> *'As a mother comforts her child, so will I comfort you...'*
> (Isaiah 66:13)

Or as Jesus himself put it, the Father will not let us down:

> *'Look at the birds of the air, they do not sow or reap or store away in barns, and yet your heavenly Father feeds them. Are you not much more valuable than they? ...And why do you worry about clothes? See how the lilies of the field grow. They do not labour or spin. Yet I tell you that not even Solomon in all his splendour was dressed like one of these. If that is how God clothes the grass of the field... will he not much more clothe you?'*   (Matthew 6:26-30)

Our heavenly Father **cannot** give us bad things:

> *'Which of you, if his son asks for bread, will give him a stone? Or if he asks for a fish, will give him a snake? If you, then, though you are evil, know how to give good gifts to*

your children, how much more will your Father in heaven
give good gifts to those who ask him?'   (Matthew 7:9-11)

Because God is different, he is always with us. As Jesus put it:

'I am with you always, even to the end of the world.'
(Matthew 28:20 LB)

He is not only **with** us, he lives inside us:

'I in them and you in me.'   (John 17:23)

Surrender

As we remember this, we come to our place of prayer with a
sense of wonder and we are humbled. This helps us to hand over
our lives to him. It also helps us to pray the prayer Jesus prayed in
Gethsemane: *'Your will, not mine, be done'* and to do what Jesus
encourages us to do: to ask:

*'Ask, and you will be given what you ask for. Seek, and you
will find. Knock, and the door will be opened.'*
(Matthew 7:7 LB)

With all this in our minds, we think back to the people I
mentioned in the Introduction to this book. I asked them the
question: 'What is prayer?' Those who said: 'Prayer is meeting
God, talking to God, trusting God, being loved, found and silent
before him,' were quite right. This is what Jesus encourages us to
believe.

3

How to
Pray

Jesus encourages us to find a quiet place where we can meet with God and he also encourages us to pray at other times – while we are walking or working, dressing or relaxing. He also teaches us what to do when we are in God's presence:

> *'"This is how you should pray."* he says.
> *"Give us today our daily bread."'* (Matthew 6:12)

Here Jesus is encouraging us to ask God to give us the things we need for the coming day: food, clothes, health, friends, support.

Since Jesus persuades us to ask for these ordinary things, we must assume that he is trying to tell us that God really cares about us. He wants to look after us just as a good earthly father or mother wants to look after the children of the family – not letting them starve or go cold or lonely or homeless. And because God is so caring, he wants us to ask: *'Ask and it will be given to you...,'* Jesus says (Matthew 7:7). *'You do not have because you do not ask,'* claims James (James 4:2).

Asking is not selfish, as some Christians seem to think. Asking puts us in a right relationship with God because it reminds us that without him our needs will not be met. It also reminds us that everything we have and everything we are is God's gift. The Bible calls this grace: We believe by grace (John 18:27). We have been saved by grace (Ephesians 2:8). Our hearts are strengthened by grace (Hebrews 13:9). By the grace of God we are what we are (1 Corinthians 15:10). His grace is all we need (2 Corinthians 12:9).

When we ask and when we receive the answers to these very

15

simple prayers, our hearts are full of thanksgiving to God. That is why, each day, I like to look ahead to the coming twenty-four hours. In a note-book, I write down the things which I think I will need during that time and I mention these things to God. The next day, as I look back, I see the way he has responded to my requests and I give him thanks.

Helping Ourselves

That is why, in chapter 1, I called prayer an adventure. But, of course, when we pray, we must not become lazy and expect God to do for us the things which we can do for ourselves. Very often he expects us to help him to become the answer to our own prayer. Like the occasion in the Gospels when the disciples warned Jesus that the crowd which had come to hear him preach and to receive his healing touch were very hungry. *'Send the crowd away so they can go to the surrounding villages and countryside and find food and lodging...'* the disciples said. But Jesus replied: *'**You** give them something to eat.'* And they did. They collected up what they could find: five little loaves and two small fish. Jesus blessed the bread and the fish, gave it back to the disciples and told **them** to give it to the people. It was while they were handing the food to the thousands of men, women and children that the miracle happened. There was enough for everyone (Matthew 14:13ff).

Praying for Others

Jesus encourages us to pray for ourselves. He also encourages us to pray for others. So he teaches us to pray, not **my** Father but **our** Father; not give **me** today **my** daily bread but give **us** today **our** daily bread.

When we look at the life of Jesus, we soon discover that such praying involves sacrifice because it means becoming involved with people – in their pain and fear. So we find Jesus leaning over a woman with a fever (Luke 4:38), touching diseased people (Luke 4:40) and even placing his hand on a leper (Luke 5:13). But as we saw in chapter 2, Jesus also kept in close touch with God – praying to him frequently.

Because he was involved with God and with men and women, he became a bridge on which God and needy people met. In the same way, we can become a bridge where God meets the people we are praying for. This happens when we keep in touch with our heavenly Father and, at the same time, become involved with people. Just being involved with people is not enough. That can be quite powerless. And just being in touch with God is not enough. That can be running away from the world. For such prayer to be effective, we need a foot in both camps – like the bridge:

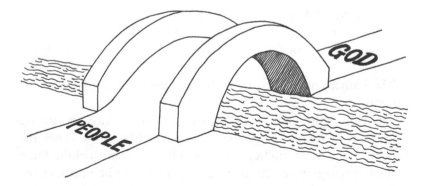

Sometimes it is hard to know how to pray for others – particularly when their stories are very sad or their problems big.

On such occasions, it can be helpful simply to recognise that, when we pray, God is with us. Aware of his presence, we can hold into his loving arms the person or the people we are concerned about in the same way as we might hold into a mother's arms her crying child recognising that she knows how best to look after her own baby.

Sometimes it helps to talk to God about the people we want to pray for. When we use words, it is very important that we do not waste time by describing the problem to God. He already knows what the problem is and what the person needs. When we pray with or without words, we should remember that Jesus is praying for that person too. He always stands at the throne of grace interceding for us (Hebrews 7:25). We therefore need to find out what he is praying for this person and echo that prayer. Any other prayer will be a waste of time and breath. Sometimes, instead of giving us words to pray, God gives us the gift of tears and we find ourselves coming into his presence and weeping – for individuals, families or national tragedies. We need to recognise these tears for what they are – a gift from God to help us to pray effectively. We also need to remember that God can translate these tears so there is no need for us to find words to go with them.

The same is true of another strange form of prayer. Paul calls it groaning:

> '*The Spirit helps us in our weakness. We do not know what we ought to pray, but the Spirit himself intercedes for us with groans that words cannot express.*' (Romans 8:26)

The Father understands this language just as well as the words we pray.

The Holy Spirit sometimes helps us in another way – by giving us the gift of tongues. Tongues is a spiritual language – not the language which our mother taught us when we were a child, but a special language given to us by God which only he understands. It is a powerful language as a brave missionary called Jackie Pullinger once discovered. God gave to Jackie a love for the drug addicts and prostitutes of Hong Kong. So she went to live in the part of the city where they lived. At first everything seemed very strange and she wondered how she could ever begin to tell these people about Jesus. One day God reminded her of the gift of tongues, so she would walk around the city every day praying in this spiritual language. This is how she described what she found:

'I learned that praying in tongues was to help people when they did not know how to pray or had run out of words. Desperate by this time to see evidence of God's power in action I began to pray privately in tongues for the dying in the Walled City. After about six weeks I noticed a difference... Extraordinary things began to happen. A gangster fell to his knees in the streets, acknowledging Jesus and weeping. Another, who had been badly beaten up, was miraculously healed... Praying in tongues was making me more sensitive to what the Holy Spirit was doing. Soon I lost count of the number of changed lives around me.'[1]

And there is another way of praying for others. It is the prayer a blind man once used when he heard the footsteps of Jesus coming his way. He cried out in a loud voice:

'Jesus, Son of David, have mercy on me!' (Mark 10:46)

Christians in the Middle East and in other countries have found that this prayer is very powerful. We can pray it for ourselves: 'Lord Jesus Christ, Son of God, have mercy on me' or we can pray it for other people: 'Lord Jesus Christ, Son of God, have mercy on my mother, have mercy on my friend, have mercy on my children, have mercy on my country.' This prayer is so simple that, like praying in tongues, we can pray it while we are working, looking after the children, shopping – or even while we are having a meal with a friend or with the family.

So prayer is not only talking to God, trusting God, being loved, found and silent before him, it also involves asking him for the things we need. When we pray the prayer of asking we need to remember that nothing is too small to bring to him, and nothing is too big. As the Angel Gabriel said to Mary:

'Nothing is impossible with God.' (Luke 1:37)

[1]Jackie Pullinger: Crack in the Wall. Hodder and Stoughton 1989, p.28.

20

4

More Ways of
Praying

We have seen that the word 'prayer' has many meanings. It is talking to God and trusting him, being loved and found by him, and being still before him. It is also surrendering to him and asking for his help for ourselves and for others. But that is not the whole story. Jesus said many other things about prayer:

> 'This, then, is how you should pray:... Forgive us the wrongs we have done, as we forgive the wrongs that others have done to us.'   (Matthew 6:12 GNB)

In other words, prayer means forgiving and receiving God's forgiveness.

We live in a fallen world where people hurt one another. Sometimes they wound others without meaning to. Sometimes they are deliberately unkind or even cruel. This means that, no matter where we live, there will be times when we feel angry or upset. At such times, it seems natural to become bitter or bad-tempered. We might even find ourselves planning to punish the person who has hurt or offended us. After all, the oldest law in the world says:

> 'If there is serious injury, you are to take life for life, eye for eye, tooth for tooth, hand for hand, foot for foot, burn for burn, wound for wound, bruise for bruise.'   (Exodus 21:23)

But, no, says Jesus. Don't think like that. Instead, pray. And when you pray, forgive the person or the people who have offended you.

This word 'forgive' really means to 'let go', to 'drop', to 'set free'. So Jesus is implying that when we pray the prayer of forgiveness, we must let go of any bitterness or hatred in our hearts. We must also drop any plans we have of punishing our enemy. Instead, we must set them free by loving them and praying for them.

Because this is a very hard thing to do, it sometimes has to happen in stages: step by step.

People sometimes suggest that to forgive means to forget. This is not true. The first step towards forgiveness is to remember, as vividly as we can, the event which has distressed us.

I think of an African lady who came to see me on one occasion. She told me that her husband had been beating her and that she was frightened to go back to him. She wanted to forgive him but she didn't know how to do it.

Forgiveness, for her, started by remembering as vividly as she could, the time when her husband treated her so cruelly. The second step is to remember that oldest law in the world: 'an eye for an eye and a tooth for a tooth'; to recognise that when someone hurts us, there is a sense in which it is our right to punish that person. So this African lady could have discussed with me ways in which she could punish her husband.

But the third step is to recognise that, as Christians, the challenge to forgive faces us with a choice: to punish or to imitate Jesus. When we sin against Jesus, he chooses to let go of his right to punish. If we are to live like him, we need to come to the place where we are prepared to drop all the accusations we have against the person who has injured us and, instead, to let God's love flow through us to them in the form of practical help!

That is the way this lady chose. When she left me, she had thought of many ways of showing her husband that she still loved him. So true forgiveness is costly and humiliating. I wonder whether this was the reason why Peter once asked Jesus:

> '"Lord, if my brother keeps on sinning against me, how many times do I have to forgive him? Seven times?" 'No, not seven times,' answered Jesus, 'but seventy times seven.'"
>
> (Matthew 18:21 GNB)

In other words, we must go on and on and on forgiving others.

Forgive

One way of doing this can be very powerful for some people. You might like to try it. If you are praying and the Holy Spirit warns you that there is some bitterness or hatred in your heart, instead of trying to pretend that it is not there, admit its existence. Admit that you are bitter or hurt because of something someone did to you. Then, aware of the presence of Jesus, let the painful memory rise to the surface of your mind. Watch what happened at the time when you were hurt.

Talk to Jesus about the hurts inside of yourself and ask him to touch and heal them just as the Good Samaritan poured oil on the wounds of the man left dying on the side of the Jerusalem to Jericho road. Tell him, too, about your feelings about the person or the people who have wounded you. Ask him to show you how he feels about those people. Ask him to give you the grace to pray the prayer he prayed from the cross when he was looking down on the people who were crucifying him: *'Father, forgive them.'* When you can truthfully pray that prayer, imagine yourself whispering to the person: 'I really forgive you from my heart.'

It may take several prayer times for you to reach the stage where you can pray such a prayer with honesty. When you can, you will feel very free.

Receive Forgiveness

When we come to the stage of forgiving others like that, something else happens. We can enter into the joyful experience of receiving God's forgiveness for ourselves.

It is always much easier to see other people's failures than our own. But we need to see ourselves for what we are. One of God's fallen people who is constantly failing him. When we have quarrelled with someone or have been hurt by someone, it is probable that we are as much to blame as they are. When we recognise this, we can come to God as we are – full of fear, coated with guilt, heavy-hearted with sorrow and shame. And we can see God as he is – full of love, longing to receive us back, over-flowing with forgiveness:

> *'If we confess our sins to God… he will forgive us our sins and purify us from all our wrongdoing.'*   (1 John 1:9 GNB)

So we can stretch out dirty hands and feel him washing us clean. We can tell him that it feels as though we have a horrible disease and we can feel him healing us and re-filling us with the energy of his Holy Spirit; filling our hands and our hearts with his love.

Worship

When we do this, joy will well up inside us and we shall discover another meaning of the word prayer. To pray is to worship.
Jesus said of worship:

> *'God is spirit, and his worshippers must worship in spirit and in truth.'*   (John 4:24)

In other words, real worship is born out of a thankful heart for when a person really worships, he or she uses their emotions, their mind and their will to praise and adore God for what he has done. That is why true, selfless worship, sorrow for sin and the determination to live a more Christ-like life so often go together.
We see this happening in the Book of Revelation. In chapter 5 we are introduced to Jesus who appears in the form of a Lamb who had once been killed. Thousands of people who had been saved by his shed blood gathered round him and worshipped by singing a new song:

> *'"Worthy is the Lamb, who was slain,*
> *to receive power and wealth and wisdom and strength and honour and glory and praise."*
> *Then I heard every creature in heaven and on earth and under the earth and on the sea, and all that is in them, singing:*

"To him who sits on the throne and to the Lamb
be praise and honour and glory and power,
for ever and ever!"'   (Revelation 5:12-14)

Every time we sin, gaze at Christ's Cross, recognize that he hung there for me, and hear him say: 'Father, forgive'; 'Father set her free', 'Father, set him free', we can sing a song of worship like that. It will come from the warmth we feel towards this God whose nature it is to set us free. It will lead us into the kind of prayer which is described in the line of a hymn some English Christians love to sing: 'Lost in wonder, love and praise.'

Spiritual Warfare

Such worship will also lead us into another form of prayer: the fight against God's Enemy, Satan himself. Some people call this kind of prayer spiritual warfare because they see it as taking part in a battle against the powers of darkness. Jesus seems to encourage this kind of prayer:

'When you pray... say... Lead us not into temptation, but deliver us from the evil one.'   (Matthew 6:13)

The verb to 'tempt' means to 'test'. And almost as soon as Jesus had been baptised, the Spirit led him into the wilderness where Satan tested him. Satan hoped that Jesus would fail the test just as Adam and Eve had done soon after the creation of the world. But Jesus did not fail. He passed.

That is not to say the test was easy. Satan waited until Jesus was tired and weak from forty days of fasting. Then he came to him and tempted him with the things humans value most: power, possessions and the opportunity to be praised by people. Each time, Jesus turned his back on the Enemy and made it quite clear that he had only one ambition in life: to do the will of God.

Jesus knew that Satan would try to make us fail. So he begs his Father to protect us from the Evil One (John 17:15). And Peter and Paul both warn us that Satan will never be far away:

'Be self-controlled and alert. Your enemy the devil prowls around like a roaring lion looking for someone to devour. Resist him, standing firm in the faith, because you know that your brothers throughout the world are undergoing the same kind of sufferings.' (1 Peter 5:8)

'Our struggle is not against flesh and blood, but against the rulers, against the authorities, against the powers of this dark world and against the spiritual forces of evil in the heavenly realms. Therefore put on the full armour of God, so that when the day of evil comes, you may be able to stand your ground, and after you have done everything, to stand.' (Ephesians 6:12, 13)

For Paul, the whole universe seemed like one big battle-ground where Christians would need to fight ungodly attitudes, sin within themselves and the invisible but powerful network of evil which Satan weaves. While he was writing about these things, he was chained to a Roman soldier. That may explain why, in his letter to the Christians in Ephesus, he suggests to them that the way to deal with Satan is to put on God's armour: the belt of truth, the breast-plate of righteousness, the shoes of peace, the shield of faith, the sword of the Spirit, God's Word and then he adds:

'And pray in the Spirit on all occasions with all kinds of prayers and requests. With this in mind, be alert and always keep on praying for all the saints.' (Ephesians 6:18)

For some people to pray 'in the Spirit' means to pray in tongues – the kind of prayer we were looking at in the last chapter. For others, to pray 'in the Spirit' means to open ourselves to God so that when he needs our prayers, the Holy Spirit can pray through us. As Paul reminds us, we must pray *'with all kinds of prayers and requests.'*

Paul also begs us to pray 'on all occasions', that is, all the time. We must pray not just when we are in our place of prayer but when we are at work or at play, in church or with family or friends. God is always with us. He has promised never ever to leave us or forsake us so we can send up prayers like arrows to him at any time of the day or night and in any place. Finally, Paul asks us to pray for one another because Satan is at work in every country in the world.

And using the Name of Jesus, we can pray with authority because Satan was defeated by the death and Resurrection of Jesus. I was reminded of this when I went on a walk on one occasion. I was about to explore a certain path when a dog started barking at me loudly and angrily. 'Be quiet!' I said in an authoritative tone of voice. Immediately, the barking stopped. 'That's just like Satan,' I thought. 'He makes a lot of noise and still has a certain amount of power but when we turn to him and say, "In the Name of the Lord Jesus Christ, be gone!", his power is broken. Jesus is Lord.'

As Lord, he encourages us to practice the prayer of forgiving, receiving forgiveness and fighting his Enemy. He also wants us to learn to listen to him.

5

Listening to God

Many Christians look very puzzled when they hear anyone suggest that they should learn to listen to God. 'But how do you do that? What does his voice sound like?' they ask.

The Bible answers that question for us. First it shows us that God is a God who speaks, and that he wants us to listen. Then it shows us that God speaks in different ways on different occasions. Sometimes he shouts (Job 37:5). At other times he whispers (1 Kings 19:12). And sometimes, although we cannot hear his voice, he speaks to us in other ways: through people and pictures, through dreams and through nature.

There is a lovely story in the Old Testament which reminds us that God's voice can be clearly heard – even by children. The story is of the boy Samuel who had been taken by his mother to live and serve God in the Temple. One night, Samuel heard God's voice calling him but he did not realise it was God. He thought it was the old priest Eli.

> 'The Lord called Samuel a third time, and Samuel got up and went to Eli and said, "Here I am; you called me." Then Eli realised that **the Lord** was calling the boy. So Eli told Samuel, "Go and lie down, and if he calls you, say, 'Speak, Lord, for your servant is listening.'" So Samuel went and lay down in his place. The Lord came and stood there, calling as at other times, "Samuel! Samuel!" Then Samuel said, "Speak, for your servant is listening."'   (1 Samuel 3:8-10)

And God told Samuel some very important state secrets.

The Old Testament is full of stories like this – of times when God spoke very clearly to his listening people. I think, for

29

example, of the way God spoke to Adam and Eve who *'heard the sound of the Lord God'* in the garden (Genesis 3:8) or of the way he came to Abraham (Genesis 12:1), Moses (Exodus 4:13), Joshua (Joshua 1:1), as well as the prophets Isaiah (Isaiah 8:1), Jeremiah (Jeremiah 7:1), Ezekiel (Ezekiel 1:3) and many others. I think, too, of the pleasure King Solomon gave to God when he was crowned King. For a coronation present, God had told him to ask for whatever he felt he would need to rule his people. Solomon said: *'Give me, O Lord, a heart that listens.'* (1 Kings 3:9). And God was pleased with the request.

We all need a heart that listens because God wants us to listen to **him**. He made this clear when he spoke on the Mount of Transfiguration. It was then that, speaking of his Son, Jesus, he said: *'This is my Son, whom I love; with him I am well pleased. **Listen to him.***' (Matthew 17:5).

Very occasionally God may speak aloud but he also speaks in many other ways.

The Bible

One of the most powerful and frequent ways God speaks to us is through his written Word, the Bible. Someone has described this book as our 'letter from home'. I like that because when I receive letters from home, from one of my children or from my mother-in-law, it is as though I can hear them talking to me through the words which they have written. We need to read the Bible in this way. It is a very long letter from Someone who loves us even more than the members of our family. This person is God.

Some Christians find that God speaks to them very powerfully when they **study** the Bible, that is, when they ask themselves certain questions while they read:

Who wrote the book of the Bible I am reading at the moment?

Why did he write it?

What kind of person did he write it for?

What would the people who were alive when he was writing think of when they read what he had written?

What would the words be saying to them?

And what do these words say to me thousands of years later?

Bible Study

Jesus made it very clear that he expects us to study the Bible – to use our minds to think carefully about what God asked people to write. But he also made it clear that the purpose of such Bible study is not so that we should have our heads full of thoughts about God but rather so that we might meet him. When I read letters from my children or a close friend, it sometimes seems as though I am meeting them because I am listening to them talk to me on paper. God wants us to meet with him. One of the doors through which we may enter is the door of Bible Study. But Jesus warns us that it is possible to **study** the Bible and fill our heads with thoughts **about** God, yet still fail to meet him:

> *'You diligently study the Scriptures because you think that by them you possess eternal life. These are the Scriptures that testify about me, yet you refuse to come to me to have life.'*
>
> (John 5:38)

Bible Meditation

Many Christians find that, when their study of the Bible leads to Bible meditation, they almost always hear God speak to them. By Bible meditation, I mean reading a few verses from the Bible as slowly as possible with one aim in mind – to hear God speak so that you can come closer to him.

Again, it is rather like reading a letter from a friend or a member of your family. When a letter comes, you read it all the way through and very often one word or one sentence stays in your memory. So you go back and read it again and again. Even when you have put the letter away, that word or sentence stays in your mind and you ponder it in the same way as Mary pondered over the many things which had happened to her (Luke 2:51).

This is the way it works for me. When I have studied a passage from the Bible in the way I have described, I read it again asking God to speak to my heart through it. (By 'the heart' the Bible means our minds and our feelings, our imagination and our memory). I then read it through slowly until a word or a phrase or a sentence seems to beg me to stop. Sometimes these words seem like new. Although I may have read them many times before, it is as though they have taken on a new importance. Sometimes it seems as though God has written them just for me for this moment in time. So I stop. I look at the words again. I say them over and over to myself until I find my heart responding. Then I talk to God about the words and listen while he talks back to me.

I think of a time when I was reading John 15. It was a time of great uncertainty in my life because my husband and I believed God was calling us to leave the church where he had been a pastor for nineteen years, but he had not yet told us where to go next. We were reading Jesus' familiar words about the vine and the branches:

> *'I am the true vine, and my Father is the gardener. He cuts off every branch in me that bears no fruit, while every branch that does bear fruit he prunes, so that it will be even more fruitful...'*   (John 15:1, 2)

The phrase *'so that it will be even more fruitful'* stopped me. I put down my Bible and said these words to myself several times. As I did so, into my mind came a picture of a real vine. I have seen them many times in the Middle East where I now live. At first, the vine in my mind's eye had many branches coming from it. They were long with many leaves on them because the grapes had only just been picked. Then, in my imagination, I watched the farmer come. He carried a pruning knife and I saw him cut off all those leafy branches. But he had not killed the vine. He had cut it back so that new branches could grow when the time was ripe. And I seemed to hear God say to me: 'I am pruning you so that you can be even more fruitful for me and for my Kingdom.' This promise filled me with great joy and love for the God who had given me such a wonderful promise just when I needed to hear it. It gave me the courage I needed to obey the Lord's command to leave that particular church. When the time came for us to say goodbye to our friends, I was still sad, of course. At the same time, I was happy because I realised that to leave was very important for God's Kingdom – leaving was part of the heavenly Gardener's pruning of my ministry and of the church.

When we meditate on the Bible, we use all the wonderful gifts God has given us: our minds so that we may understand, the eyes of our imagination so that we may see, the ears of our heart so that we may hear God speaking to us, our memories so that God's words may heal and comfort and strengthen us and our feelings so that we may respond to him.

Bible meditation takes time but it is time very well spent – especially for those, who, like the boy Samuel, are praying: *'Speak, Lord, your servant is listening.'*

Bible meditation is part of listening prayer. Its great value is that it helps us to feed on God's Word – to eat it. Jesus implies that this is what we are meant to do with it:

> *'"Man does not live on bread alone", but on every word that comes from the mouth of God.'*   (Matthew 4:4)

When we meditate, we take spiritual food into our mouth through reading the words of Scripture. Then we chew them by turning them over in our mind. Finally, we swallow them by pondering them and letting the hidden truths travel from our heads into our hearts.

Other People

God not only speaks through the written Word, he speaks through the Living Word, his Son Jesus. It is very important that we learn to meditate on the life and teaching of Jesus. This way, God will speak powerfully to us at every stage of our life – changing our way of thinking as well as our way of living.

And he speaks to us through people. We see a beautiful example of this in Acts 9. Jesus has just appeared to Saul of Tarsus. Saul goes into Damascus to wait for Jesus to tell him what he is to do next. He had to be led into the city by his friends because the light surrounding Jesus had blinded him.

Saul knew that Jesus could speak to him directly. He had already heard him say: *'I am Jesus, whom you are persecuting.'* (Acts 9:6). But he was to learn that God also speaks to us through other people:

> *'In Damascus there was a disciple named Ananias. The Lord called to him in a vision, "Ananias!" "Yes, Lord." he answered. The Lord told him, "Go to the house of Judas on Straight Street and ask for a man from Tarsus named Saul, for he is praying. In a vision he has seen a man named Ananias come and place his hands on him to restore his sight."... Then Ananias went to the house and entered it. Placing his hands on Saul, he said, "Brother Saul, the Lord – Jesus, who appeared to you on the road as you were coming here – has sent me so that you may see again and be filled with the Holy Spirit."'* (Acts 9:10-17)

And we all know how powerfully Saul, or Paul as we know him, was used by God after that.

God still uses people to speak to us. A letter reminded me of this while I was writing this chapter. The letter was from a girl who had sat next to me in church a few months earlier. I didn't know her but she reminded me that that day, in the middle of the service, she had started to cry because she couldn't believe in God and she was frightened. 'You listened, sympathised, talked and helped and were one of several people God used to help me to find him,' her letter said. 'So I'll always be grateful.'

6

More Ways of
Listening to God

At the end of the last chapter, we looked at the way God used Ananias to speak to Paul soon after Paul's conversion. If we look carefully at the verses I quoted, we will see that God does not only speak to us directly or through the Bible or through other people. He has many other ways of making himself heard.

Luke makes it clear that he sometimes speaks to us through pictures. As he explained to Ananias:

> 'Go to the house of Judas on Straight Street and ask for a man from Tarsus named Saul, for he is praying. In a vision he has seen a man named Ananias come and place his hand on him to restore his sight.' (Acts 9:11, 12)

In Bible times, God very often spoke through pictures or visions and dreams. A vision is a picture or short film which we see with our imagination while we are awake and listening to the Holy Spirit. A dream is a picture or short film which we see with our imagination when we are asleep. Whether we are awake or asleep, God shows us these pictures for one reason: because he wants to tell us something important.

So God spoke to Peter through a vision while he was praying on the roof of his house:

> 'He saw heaven opened and something like a large sheet being let down to earth by its four corners. It contained all kinds of four-footed animals, as well as reptiles of the earth and birds of the air. Then a voice told him, "Get up, Peter. Kill and eat." "Surely not, Lord!" Peter replied. "I have never eaten anything impure or unclean." (Acts 10:10-14)

Peter was a Jew. He thought the Gospel was only for Jews. Through this powerful picture, God set him free from this thinking and showed him that the Gospel was for people of every tribe and language and nation. And the timing of the vision was very important. A Gentile was on his way to see Peter at the same time as God was giving Peter the vision. As a result of this message in picture language, Peter was to bring this man into the Kingdom of God.

God also spoke very powerfully through dreams. After the wise men had left Mary, Joseph and the baby Jesus, for example, God spoke to Joseph in a dream:

> 'When they had gone, an angel of the Lord appeared to Joseph in a dream. "Get up," he said, "take the child and his mother and escape to Egypt. Stay there until I tell you, for Herod is going to search for the child to kill him."'

> (Matthew 2:13)

Dreams

God still speaks through visions and dreams today. As he promised through the prophet Joel, it is one of the gifts the Holy Spirit brings with him:

> 'In the last days, God says, I will pour out my Spirit on all people. Your sons and daughters will prophesy, your young men will see visions, your old men will dream dreams. Even on my servants, both men and women, I will pour out my Spirit in those days, and they will prophesy. I will show wonders in the heaven above and signs on the earth below...'
> (Quoted Acts 2:17-19)

Nature

God not only speaks through visions and dreams, he also speaks through nature. The Psalmist reminds us of this:

'The heavens declare the glory of God;
the skies proclaim the work of his hands.
Day after day they pour forth speech;
night after night they display knowledge.
There is no speech or language
where their voice is not heard.
Their voice goes out into all the earth,
their words to the ends of the world.'   (Psalm 19:1-4)

And I was reminded of it while I was writing this chapter. I was staying in a small cottage in the English countryside at the time. Temperatures had fallen below zero. When I went downstairs to make my breakfast, a small tree outside the window was bright white. It was as though, in the night, someone had covered every branch and twig with frost. 'What does that tree say to you?' I asked my husband. 'It shouts to me one word: Glory. The glory of God.'

Of course, the tree cannot speak words which we can hear. But, as the Psalmist rightly points out, the wonders which God has created: the starry night sky, sunsets and sunrises, mountains and rivers, and oceans and trees all speak a silent language. People all over the world can hear it when the Holy Spirit opens their eyes and ears. Then this beauty points them to the Creator: God.

Prophecy

God also speaks through the gift of prophecy. As we have already seen, the prophet Joel warned us that this would happen: *'Your sons and daughters will prophesy...'*

When the Holy Spirit gives a word of prophecy to Christians today, it may not be saying anything about the future but rather about the present. The word of prophecy is a message from God, given through one of his disciples, but inspired by the Holy Spirit to encourage and strengthen other Christians or a whole church.

Usually, the word of prophecy is given by God at a certain time and it is so powerful and important that there is no need to write it down. It is obvious that God has spoken. But, occasionally, God seems to tell someone to write the words down.

A pastor in England felt God telling him to do this with the words which he was hearing. He published the prophecies in a little book called "I Am With You". I read a few lines from this book most days and am sometimes very surprised by the way God so obviously speaks to me through the words I read there.

I think of the time when my husband and I were beginning to recognise that God was calling us to move from the church where we had served for nineteen years. One morning, when I was feeling rather frightened by the idea, I read these words: 'There will be times when you will not see the immediate way ahead. You may be filled with panic, wanting to avoid what could be a disastrous step. Remember you do not always need to see the road ahead. It is sufficient, for the moment, to see ME!

When the time is right for a choice to be made you will know and I will assist you through it. Until that time be sure that merely keeping close to Me guarantees your moving in the right direction, despite questions and doubts raging in your mind.

When you cannot see clearly the next step, there is a good reason for My withholding that awareness... Do not feel the awful responsibility for choosing your path when that is not necessary for the moment. Just hide in Myself and know that you will soon see clearly... Until then, you are precisely where I want you to be.'[1]

These words gave me the courage I needed to go on and I was very thankful to God for giving the words to this pastor.

The Word of Knowledge

Just as God sends messages to his people through the word of prophecy, so he still seems to speak to day through the word of knowledge. The word of knowledge means a little piece of information about a person which we could not receive from reading a book or even talking to others about them. The word of knowledge may tell us where they are, for example or show us how they are feeling at this moment in time.

Jesus was given a word of knowledge when he was talking to

the Samaritan woman at the well. She told Jesus that she had no husband. Through a word of knowledge, he saw that she had had five husbands. When she heard him say this, she was very surprised and believed that he was the Messiah (John 4:18).

The Word of Wisdom

Through the Holy Spirit, God is still giving Christians today words of prophecy and words of knowledge. He also trusts us with the gift of wisdom. This gift is very valuable because it helps us to make right decisions and to say the right word at the right time.

King Solomon was given this gift right at the beginning of his reign. So when two women came to him with a terrible problem, he knew what to say to them.

The two women brought two babies with them. One was alive, the other was dead. Both mothers said that the live baby was **her** baby. They asked Solomon to decide which one of them was telling the truth.

Many of us would not have known how to deal with this problem, but Solomon used the gift of wisdom and ordered that the live baby should be cut in two. Both mothers could then have half of it. The real mother quickly said 'no'. She would rather see her baby live even if it meant that the other woman would take care of the child. Her choice helped Solomon to discover that she was the real mother and that the other woman was lying (1 Kings 3:7-9).

Ordinary Things

Jesus shows us that his Father speaks to us, not only through these special and valuable gifts of the Holy Spirit, but through ordinary things as well. One spring day, when he walked through the fields with his disciples, he noticed that the ground was covered with tiny, coloured flowers. These reminded him of the faithfulness of God so he used them to teach his disciples not to worry:

'Do not worry about your life, what you will eat or drink; or about your body, what you will wear... Why do you worry about clothes? See how the lilies of the field grow. They do not labour or spin. Yet I tell you that not even Solomon in all his splendour was dressed like one of these. If that is how God clothes the grass of the field, which is here today and tomorrow is thrown into the fire, will he not much more clothe you, O you of little faith?' (Matthew 6:25, 28)

In the same way, his stories are almost always about ordinary things and people: yeast, vines, farmers, trees, snakes, scorpions, pearls, women sweeping their houses, children playing in the market place and so on.

It is important that we recognise the way in which God normally speaks to his people because listening to God is a vital part of prayer. One reason is that, every moment of every day and night, Jesus is praying for us and his world. The writer to the Hebrews makes this very clear when he says:

'He always lives to intercede for [us].' (Hebrews 7:25)

When we pray for people or situations, it is as though Jesus gives us the honour of standing alongside him in his Father's presence and becoming his prayer partner. So it is essential that we should discover how he is praying for these people or problems or situations. When we have discovered the mind of Christ, our prayer becomes an echo of his prayer. If we never stop to listen, we might be praying a different prayer from Jesus and that would be a waste of time, energy and breath.

[1]John Woolley – "I Am With You". Crown (Great Britain) 1991. p.18.

7

The Holy Spirit
and Prayer

We have seen in earlier chapters of this book that prayer is, among other things, talking to God and listening to him, forgiving others and being forgiven, worshipping God and meeting with him. Prayer also includes asking for things for ourselves and for other people and fighting God's enemy, Satan. Prayer is a gift of the Holy Spirit.

The Holy Spirit not only gives us the gift of prayer, he helps us to use this gift. He is able to do this because, as Jesus puts it, he is 'another Comforter' (John 14:26).

The word for 'Comforter' which Jesus uses here also means an Advocate or a Counsellor – that is someone who knows how to help another person when they are in need. Just as we might ask a doctor to come alongside a sick person, we are invited to ask for the Holy Spirit's help whenever we try to pray.

The word 'another' also means 'one of the same kind'. By using this word Jesus seems to be assuring us that the Helper, the Holy Spirit, is just like himself.

Tells us we are God's Children

Paul shows us how this Christ-like Holy Spirit helps every Christian to pray. In his letter to the Romans, he puts it this way:

> 'For his Holy Spirit speaks to us deep in our hearts, and tells us that we really are God's children.'   (Romans 8:16 LB)

He goes on to show us that it is by the grace given to us by God's Spirit that we find ourselves able to call God 'Abba' –

'Father'. This is good news for every Christian. In particular, it is good news for those who find it difficult to think of God as 'Father' because their earthly father did not love them in the way they needed to be loved. It means that we do not have to come to God in our own strength to do what Jesus suggested: *'When you pray say, "Abba", "Daddy"'*.

Instead, the Holy Spirit will pour into us all the grace and strength, courage, love and healing we need, to come to God in the same way as little children come to a good father – full of love and trust. This is possible for every Christian because the Holy Spirit also pours the love of God deep into the heart of the believer:

> *'We know how dearly God loves us, and we feel this warm love everywhere within us because God has given us the Holy Spirit to fill our hearts with this love.'* (Romans 5:5 LB)

It is good news, too, for those who cannot enjoy the motherly qualities of God because their earthly mother did not give them the warmth, tenderness and gentleness they needed. The Holy Spirit fills us with such tenderness that old hurts are healed, darkness becomes light, despair is turned to hope and we experience joy even in times of sorrow.

Helps us in our Weakness

In the same letter to the Christians in Rome, Paul goes on to show that the Holy Spirit helps us in other ways. We are weak. So often we do not know what to pray for, which words to use or how to say them. The Holy Spirit who lives inside every believer knows this. Happily, he does know how to pray. He helps us by praying for us and in us. This is also good news because the Father understands the Holy Spirit's prayers and answers them. It is good news, too, because the Holy Spirit knows the Father as well as he knows us and so he knows just the right prayers to pray – asking for things the Father wants to give us:

*'The Holy Spirit helps us... with our praying. For we don't
even know what we should pray for, nor how to pray as we
should; but the Holy Spirit prays for us with such feeling
that it cannot be expressed in words. And the Father who
knows all hearts knows, of course, what the Spirit is saying
as he pleads for us in harmony with God's own will.'*

(Romans 8:26, 27 LB)

In other words, the Holy Spirit prays in us and for us and
through us and with us. We never pray alone but always in
partnership with him.

Shows us the Way to the Father

In another letter – his letter to the Christians in Ephesus – Paul
reminds us that the Holy Spirit is the One who shows us the way
into the Father's presence:

*'Now all of us, whether Jews or Gentiles, may come to God
the Father with the Holy Spirit's help because of what Christ
has done for us.'*   (Ephesians 2:18)

We need this help because we cannot come to God through our
mind nor through our feelings nor through our body. We can only
come to him through our spirit. As Jesus put it:

*'The time... has now come when true worshippers will
worship the Father in spirit and truth, for they are the kind
of worshippers the Father seeks. God is spirit, and his
worshippers must worship in spirit and in truth.'*

(John 4:23, 24)

It is the Holy Spirit who links our spirit with God himself.
When I am trying to explain this to people, I sometimes liken it to
the time when the wife of the American Ambassador in Paris
invited me to meet her. 'Come to the gate of the Embassy,' she

said, 'and mention your name. The security guards will then open the gates and doors for you.' I arrived at the time we had agreed, mentioned my name and, sure enough, doors which are not normally opened to the public for security reasons were opened to me. But when I was shown inside the huge building, I would not have found my way to the Ambassador's apartment unless a friend had met me inside the front door and led the way.

The Holy Spirit is like that friend who met me at the door and led me along the long corridors which took me right into the presence of the Ambassador's wife.

The Holy Spirit leads us right into the presence of Jesus himself.

Helps us to Worship

The Holy Spirit is also the one who helps us to worship. Jesus warns us that without the Spirit we shall never be able truly to give God the honour and praise he deserves:

> 'God is Spirit, and we must have his help to worship as we should.' (John 4:24 LB)

The reason why we need the Holy Spirit's help when we worship is that true worship comes from hearts that have been warmed to the love of God. As we have already seen, it is the Holy Spirit who lights the flame of love in our hearts which results in us adoring God, singing his praises and feeling full of wonder because of who he is and what he has done. It is the Holy Spirit, too, who persuades us to offer God everything we have and everything we are – to give to him the worship of grateful lives.

He Changes Us

When we offer God our lives, the Holy Spirit does for us a miracle which we could not do ourselves. He changes us. As Paul puts it in his letter to the Galatians:

'When the Holy Spirit controls our lives he will produce this kind of fruit in us: love, joy, peace, patience, kindness, goodness, faithfulness, gentleness and self control.'

(Galatians 5:22 LB)

Paul continues:

'If we are living now by the Holy Spirit's power, let us follow the Holy Spirit's leading in every part of our lives.'

(Galatians 5:25 LB)

To change and be changed like this is a part of our prayer. As someone has put it, to pray is to change.

None of us can manufacture these Christ-like qualities for ourselves. They grow in us as the Holy Spirit takes over more and more of our lives and changes us into the likeness of Jesus. This realisation keeps us humble and trusting. It rescues us from false pride. It underlines for us that everything we have and everything we are, is a pure gift from God. And it reveals to us the miracle of prayer – that, very slowly and gradually, it changes us.

When we recognise for ourselves what an important part the Holy Spirit plays in our prayer, we recognise, too, that we need to ask God every day to fill us with this Spirit. Christians all over the world do this when they sing a song like this:

'Spirit of the living God,
Fall afresh on me.
Break me, melt me, mould me, fill me.
Spirit of the living God,
Fall afresh on me.'

When we pray a prayer like that, we can be certain that God **will** give us a fresh touch of his lift-giving, prayerful Spirit. He wants us to draw near to him far more than we want to come into his presence. So he makes it easy for us to come. And Jesus promises that the Father will never say no to this prayer:

'If you, then, though you are evil, know how to give good

45

gifts to your children, how much more will your Father in heaven give the Holy Spirit to those who ask him?'

(Luke 11:13)

The Holy Spirit not only changes us, he works miracles when we pray. We see a wonderful example of the way prayer changes things and people in John's Gospel. Jesus and his disciples were attending a wedding party. Mary, Jesus' mother, was there too. When Mary discovered that the host had run out of wine, she realised that he would be feeling full of shame and embarrassment. So she went to Jesus and simply said: *'They have no wine.'* This simple prayer produced the first miracle Jesus ever did in public.

Our prayer can produce similar miracles, not because of who we are nor because of the words we use, but because of who God is: the Faithful One who wants his people to enjoy peace, that deep sense of well-being God loves to fill us with.

In the first chapter of this book, I described prayer as a journey into God. I suggested that, as you read the book, you would pray for God's grace to make that journey. Just before I finished this chapter, I read an article on prayer which someone else has written. In it, he suggested that prayer is rather like a very big cart wheel. The centre of the wheel, the hub, is like the quietness I described in the early chapters of this book. The outside of the wheel, the rim, is like our everyday life when we have to keep in

touch with the world around us. The spokes are the many, many ways of praying. These hold quietness and busyness together. They help us to be aware of God both when we are being quiet and when we are busy.

The cartwheel of your life began its journey towards God before you began reading this book. It will move on now that you have reached the last page. As we continue to travel towards God, we still need to pray that prayer the disciples prayed:

"Lord, teach us to pray."

❖ ❖ ❖ ❖

If you have enjoyed this book and would like to help us to send a copy of it and many other titles to needy pastors in the **Third World**, please write for further information or send your gift to:

Sovereign World Trust, P.O. Box 777, Tonbridge, Kent TN11 0ZS, United Kingdom

or to the **'Sovereign World'** distributor in your country. If sending money from outside the United Kingdom, please send an International Money Order or Foreign Bank Draft in STERLING, drawn on a **UK** bank to **Sovereign World Trust**.